D1794876

# THE
# JOSEPH CHRONICLES

*An epic that changed the world*

## Mal Fletcher

**Next Wave International™**

**Copyright © 1998, 2003 Mal Fletcher**
All rights reserved.

This edition published by Next Wave International™
Visit our website at www.nextwaveonline.com

No part of this publication may be reproduced, stored in a retrieval system, or transmitted, in any form or by any means, electronic or mechanical, including photocopy, recording or any information storage and retrieval system, without the prior written permission of the publisher, nor be otherwise circulated in any form of binding or cover other than that in which it is published and without a similar condition being imposed on the subsequent purchaser.

ISBN 0-9579020-4-2

1. Youth    2. Christian Witness    3. Youth Leadership

Unless otherwise stated, Scripture quotations are from the New International Version of the Bible, copyright 1973, 1978, and 1984 by International Bible Society.

Printed and bound in Australia

Cover Art: Dan Chattaway, X Media Design
Layout: Hanne Andreasen

Next Wave International™
Drejervej 11-21, 2400-Copenhagen NV, Denmark
**admin@nextwaveonline.com**

And

255 Old South Road, Reynella S.A., 5161, Australia
**gary@nextwaveonline.com**

**Don't forget to check out:**

# www.nextwaveonline.com

- Daily Recharge: get your faith charged up everyday with Mal Fletcher
- Books
- E-books
- MP3 audio files: Mal's hot teaching on a range of subjects
- Audio CDs
- Articles: Mal Fletcher writes provocatively on major issues
- News about what Next Wave International™ is doing, including coming events
- Sign up for the monthly E-News: including V-News with Mal
- And more…

PDA version now available

# www.edges.tv

- Watch programs online: broadband or modem connection
- Transcripts and research material: a great resource for study assignments etc.
- Info about the Bible, Jesus and Christianity
- How you can get involved with EDGES
- Sign up for the monthly EDGES Update: all the news on this pioneer program
- Become an EDGES partner… and speak into 200 nations!
- And more…

---

*Tell your friends!*
*The Joseph Chronicles is also available as an*
## E-BOOK
www.nextwaveonline.com

---

# THE JOSEPH CHRONICLES

*An epic that changed the world*

# LEVEL I

# That Dreamer
## [Or Nightmare in Father's House]

*Early in her career, Madonna was the rock star of choice for people who liked wearing their underwear on the outside!*

*She carved her niche in an already overcrowded music marketplace using, among other things, the power of shock.*

A few years back, MTV produced a program that was devoted to this question: 'What makes a really hard-core Madonna fan tick?'

The responses from some of her most ardent followers were more revealing than some of Madonna's old outfits!

These people had come together from all walks of life, from places far and wide, but they all had one thing in common. Their lives revolved almost entirely around a fixation on the 'material girl'.

In wrapping up the program, the editors gave the last say to a young woman who claimed to be 'Madonna's number one fan'.

'What separates a real fan from a pretender?' she was asked.

'A real fan is willing to drop everything to be where Madonna is,' she replied. 'Even if that means leaving a home, a job, a friendship or even a lover.'

## Newsflash...

In the age in which we live, people are looking for leadership - *big time*!

As a Christian, I believe that the greatest leader who ever walked this planet was a man who was born into obscurity.

He grew up in a town of no more than five hundred people and, with the exception of one trip to Egypt as a boy, he never travelled more than eighty miles from his hometown. Yet he went on to change the world forever, more than any other person before or since. And in just three years of public life.

He apparently had no political agenda, no axe to grind for the 'left' or the 'right'. He was not interested in fame or fortune. In fact, he openly warned his followers about the dangers of both.

He stood up for the oppressed and the downtrodden, particularly those who were made so by an unfeeling religious system.

His teaching was revolutionary, captivating and inspiring. He emphasized the idea that God is not just some distant figure whom we may fear but can never really know. He is, above all else, a Father at heart - one who sent his Son to rescue wayward humanity; to bring all who are willing back into his family.

This kind of philosophy came as a welcome surprise to people who'd come to see God only as a hanging judge.

**In the age in which we live, people are looking for leadership.**

Because it was so radical and so liberating to people who received it, his teaching eventually brought down on him the wrath of powerful figures in the religious ruling class. They envied his popularity. They knew better than anyone just how radical his teaching really was, and what a danger it posed to their godless and greedy way of life.

In the end, it all led him to the ignominy and agony of death by Roman crucifixion.

## It Isn't Over Yet...

Today, he is still changing lives, not just through the truth and sincerity of his words or the force of his personality, but through his real here-and-now-power to heal sick bodies, to bring peace to troubled minds, and to give meaning to truly lost souls (see Luke 4:18). Over two millennia ago, he started a mission to change the world and he's still doing it - with greater impact than ever before!

Wherever people gather in his name his power and presence are being made manifest. Even if it's just in two's and three's, and even in places where governments openly oppose Christian faith, like China. All over the world, God is attesting to the witness of his followers, working miracles in his name.

Not long before his death, Napoleon Bonaparte made the following comment: 'Alexander, Charlemagne and myself all founded world empires. On what did we rest the creations of our genius? Upon force.'

'Only Jesus Christ founded an empire built upon love and today there are millions of men around the world who would gladly lay down their lives for him.'

H. G. Wells was not just a science fiction author; he was first and foremost an historian. And he was not a Christian. He said that, for an historian, the measure of a man's greatness is what he leaves behind him to grow when he dies. By that standard, said Wells, Jesus comes first in all of history.

## More Than A Club

The strength of Jesus' leadership is still being felt in the world today.

Through the presence of his Spirit in their lives, his growing band of followers carries the torch of his light and love as a beacon of hope in a dark and weary world.

The spirit of leadership that rested on Jesus the Man no longer rests on just one person. It now resides in a whole community, one that comprises people from every race, tribe and language group on the planet.

Jesus didn't come to form a club, or to build an organisation. He launched something quite unique. It's called the church.

No, not the institutional establishment we often *call* the church, with its grandiose buildings and layers of stultifying tradition built up over centuries. The real church is simply the community of all real believers, those for whom Jesus is personal Saviour and Lord of their daily lives. These are the ones who really do take up their cross daily to follow him (see Mark 8:34).

Local churches, missions and ministries each have leaders of their own. Yet, these people recognise that they are merely under-shepherds. Ultimately, there is only one who can be called the leader of the church, and only one who builds the church. That's Jesus himself (see Matthew 16:18).

## Big Plans

'Make no little plans,' wrote D. H. Burham. 'They have no magic to stir man's blood. Make big plans; aim high in hope and word.'

When Jesus calls people to follow him, he doesn't invite them to take part in some small, insignificant work. He doesn't ask them to play Trivial Pursuit with their lives. He invites them to become a part of a world-changing force!

'You are the salt of the earth,' he says to them. 'You are the light of the world - like a city on a mountain, glowing in the night for all to see' (see Matthew 5:13-14).

Jesus calls his people to take up a position of *influence* in society, to become *world-changers* by allowing the reality of a living Christ to permeate their every word, work and relationship.

This kind of influence is quite different to worldly power. Power tends to corrupt people, because it carries with it all kinds of attractive but dangerous trappings. Power seduces people, dulling their spiritual senses, turning them into 'self-made' individuals who think they have no need of God.

**When Jesus calls people to follow him, he invites them to become a part of a world-changing force!**

Power also has a way of killing the servant's heart, the attitude of putting others before self. According to Jesus, a servant attitude should be one of the major things that sets his people apart from the crowd (see Matthew 20:25-26).

Charles Finney, the great revivalist, is said to have turned more than one million people to Christ during his lifetime - way before the advent of mass media and communications technology. He once remarked that, 'The church of Jesus Christ was first instituted to be a body of reformers.'

People in our age are hungry for leadership, for role models who are worth emulating and for values that actually work. It's time for Jesus' people everywhere to become the influence for good - for God - that they were called to be.

No other generation has had such an opportunity to do just that! Think about it. This Millennial generation has before it unprecedented opportunities for travel, global communication, technological advancement and education. With the prevalence of mass media and the ubiquitous Internet, Millennials are far more aware of global issues than any previous generation of young people.

There are also some great spiritual renewals taking place around the world today. What a generation you're living in! What a chance your generation has to change things.

# 'That Dreamer!'

Even if you've never read the Bible, chances are you've heard about Joseph. He was the dude with the amazing Technicolor dream coat. Stage shows and animated movies are made about him.

But at Level 1 of the Joseph Chronicles, he was anything but a popular pin-up boy occupying centre stage. The real Joseph lived a long while before the West End, Broadway or Hollywood ever existed. He was part of the early history of the Egyptian empire.

With the aid of that wonderful time machine known as literary license, let's take ourselves back to those bygone days...

## Long, Long Ago In A Galaxy Not So Far Away...

As our epic opens, Joseph is born into a small, second-class race of people who live in the shadow of the unparalleled power of the Pharaohs.

A Jewish nation is still a thing of the future. In Joseph's time, the 'nation' consists of around one hundred and twenty people. It is basically just a large extended family - they can all still get together for the family Christmas party!

The Egyptians, the ruling super-class of the day, consider the Hebrews to be such a lowly group that they won't even eat with them. Dining with the sons of Abraham is considered 'detestable' to the fine, cultured citizens of Egypt (see Genesis 43:42).

Joseph is working as a shepherd. It's a second-class job, but it's the only thing available to him. In these times, shepherds are often looked upon with suspicion (see Genesis 46:34). They're seen in much the same way as insurance salesmen and used car merchants will be seen in much later times.

Young Joe is the second-to-last in a large family of brothers and he just happens to be his father's favourite son. He can hardly be blamed for that - his mother was dad's favourite *wife* - but it sets him up for a tough time at the hands of his older and very competitive siblings.

To make matters worse, Joseph is inclined to have very potent and colourful dreams. In these days, dreams are seen as windows into the future and the ability to dream is often a prized gift - along with the gift of interpreting dreams.

Joseph's visions are special effects blockbusters - real Industrial Light and Magic stuff. If Joseph's brothers don't already resent him for being dad's favourite, they soon come to hate the message suggested by his dreams.

Though it comes in different forms, Joseph's recurring vision always ends the same way. Joseph is exalted to a position of prominence and influence while his brothers bow in obeisance before him. Not the kind of dream to help you win friends and influence people, especially if most of your own family already despises you...

Predictably, Joe's dream turns into a nightmare around the home. His father can't grasp it at all, and his brothers look for the first available chance to get rid of this kid with the attitude!

> **It's time for Jesus' people everywhere to become the influence that they were called to be.**

One day, when Joseph is in his late teens, the brothers see their big chance. Joseph is coming toward them in the fields well out of dear daddy's reach. Looking up, one of the brothers cynically remarks, 'Hey, here comes that dreamer...'.

Now, those words can be used as either a compliment or an insult. In our own times, most people recognise that great achievements always begin with great dreamers.

A generation after it was first given, we are still celebrating the speech of Rev. Martin Luther King Jnr. He had a dream. He articulated a vision that was shared by most fair-minded people of his generation; a vision for a society where people were treated fairly and, in the unforgettable words of King, children are 'judged not by the colour of their skin but by the content of their character.'

There is still much to be done in the reconciliation of races in downtown America, but positive changes have been made. King's speech still stands as a landmark in the struggle for ethnic equality and a beacon of hope for all who long for a just world. A dream can be a potent force for change.

Henry Ford said that, 'The poor man is not that man without a penny. The poor man is that man without a dream.'

Sadly, so many people feel too hurt, let down, insecure or bitter to accommodate or celebrate the good dreams of others. So it was in Joseph's time. Back to the story...

## Sold... To The Man With The Whip

Joseph's brothers, their thoughts fuelled by the fires of jealousy and revenge, assault him, throw him into a pit and then proceed to sell him off to a group of passing merchants. It's a kind of slavery-cult-deal. Young Joe is whisked off to who-knows-where without even a chance to pack a toothbrush.

To add insult to injury, the conspiratorial brothers tell Joseph's doting father that wild animals have killed him. It breaks the old man's heart.

If you read the full Joseph Chronicles all the way to Level 4 you will find that Joseph *never* loses sight of his God-given dream. He never gives up on the calling he received as a teenager growing up in a dysfunctional home. Right from the start he is surrounded by cynics yet he remains totally committed to that vision of his future.

There are times on his journey when Joseph must feel that his dream will never become a reality. But he holds on, despite the way things appear. He's still holding on when, finally, everything in his life takes a sudden and dramatic change for the better.

He ends up co-ruling a nation and heading up one of the most significant international aid efforts in ancient history! But more on that later...

## Dream On...

So, lesson number one for us is this: if God gives you a dream, don't let it die.

No matter how young you are when you start dreaming... No matter *how* loud the voices of your critics... No matter how many people or situations seem to be set against your vision... No matter how long the dream takes in making its way to you... Stay with the program!

Remember: nobody ever built a statue to a cynic. It's only the *believers*, the *dreamers* and *doers* that we celebrate.

You have a choice to make, right now. It's one of the most fundamental of all decisions and will shape the rest of your life. Will you become a dreamer or will you, like so many in this age, become a cynic, a doubter, a 'could-have-been'?

There's something else worth noting about Joseph. His dream isn't something that popped into his head while he was smoking funny green cigarettes. It's not something he borrowed from the latest self-help book. No, his dream has been handed to him *by revelation from God.*

That's the kind of dream you *can* hold onto, through thick and thin. Why? Because God is unchanging - the Bible often calls him 'the Rock' (see Psalm 31:3; 62:3).

God's not about to be swayed by circumstances on this earth and he's not going to be defeated by the schemes of men. The dreams *he* gives you for your life are a *sure thing.* But there's a price: you must be willing to follow his dream more than your own, even if it makes you unpopular.

That's what Jesus meant when he said, 'If any of you wants to be my follower, you must put aside your selfish ambition, shoulder your cross, and follow me' (Mark 8:34).

Notice: Jesus doesn't play *Who Wants to be a Millionaire?* or *Let's Make A Deal.* He doesn't say, 'Hey, here's an idea - let's do *my* thing for half the week, and then *your* thing for the other half!' No, the call Jesus makes is more dangerous than that. He demands all or nothing. He doesn't ask, he commands. He says, 'You follow, I lead! Period!'

**If God gives you a dream, don't let it die.**

Denying yourself means totally abandoning everything you were before Jesus entered your life; leaving behind your old values, attitudes and hurts. Yes, even your old dreams, ambitions and plans. Taking up your cross means finding what God wants for your life and doing it, even though it *will* cost you everything.

So, if it's just *your* dream that's filling your mind, it may *need* to die. But once you've laid hold of God's dream for your life, you just can't afford to let it expire.

Mother Teresa is revered today, all around the world. During her eventful life, she won the respect of presidents and kings and even key people in the mass media, who are often so sceptical about anything remotely 'religious'. What gave this small Albanian nun such favour? As a young woman, she left a cushy job teaching at a middle class school and committed herself to the poorest of the poor. She denied herself and took up her cross in

Jesus' name. God's dreams for her took time to fulfil, but he gave her much greater influence than she could ever have imagined.

God's dreams for you can be trusted. Your dreams for yourself cannot. Revelation 1:8 tells us: '[The Lord God says] I am the Alpha and the Omega - the beginning and the end... I am the one who is, who always was, and who is still to come, the Almighty One.'

God, your Father, sees the whole sweep of history as if it were one long, seamless *now*. He is not restricted by the parameters of time and space. He not only sees *the* future, he sees *your* future.

You can only see the present and remember a fraction of the past. You're only aware of the things others have told you about yourself, or what your circumstances and environment have suggested about you. God knows what you're *really* capable of doing - in his power. He sees it all because he *is* the Alpha and Omega, the beginning and the end.

That's why the apostle Paul wrote, 'By his mighty power at work within us, [God] is able to accomplish infinitely more than we would ever dare to ask or hope' (Ephesians 3:20).

## Not Big Enough...

God was conscious of you before you were even born. He had made a unique space for you in his scheme for planet earth. He was there when you took your first faltering steps as a Christian, and he will be there to carry you over the finish line.

Basically, though, God is not interested in fulfilling *your* dreams at all. Why not? Because they're much too small, they're way too limited for what he has in mind!

At the end of his story, we find our enterprising hero Joseph feeding whole nations at a time of desperate hunger. He is rescuing cities while his brothers are struggling just to feed their families.

He becomes a gracious, merciful and compassionate international leader who uses his exalted position of influence to rescue many thousands of people from certain starvation.

It all starts with a dream - but not Joseph's dream. He doesn't sit down and work out ten goals or ten steps to take him to political power. The whole adventure begins with *God* speaking to Joseph. It's God who takes the initiative. At the time, Joseph isn't even looking for the kind of dream God has in store for him.

For Joseph's part, he receives the dream and makes the

decision to believe it and to act as if it *will happen* - just because God says it will.

That's what the Bible calls 'faith': believing things God has said to and about you simply because God has said them! Faith dares to act as if God is a person of his word, as if his promises *are* on their way to you - even if everyone and everything around you seems to be against them.

A few years ago, a young woman in Canada told me that God had promised her she would one day be the Prime Minister of her nation. Normally, people who say things like that are a little unhinged in the cranial department, but I could see that this was a well-presented and intelligent young woman. She had really thought about this. Still, it was a pretty audacious thing to believe.

> **Once you've laid hold of God's dream for your life, you just can't afford to let it expire.**

Many people would have scoffed at her announcement. Some people would have said, 'Pigs might fly...' But I've read the story of Joseph a time or two, and I know that weird, unexpectedly great things *can* happen for people who believe what God puts in their hearts.

Whether she'll ever be Prime Minister, I can't say. Whether or not God *did* give her this dream, I don't really know. But I *do* know that those who dare to dream in this generation of cynics will always be the ones who are destined to lead and to have a great influence on their generation.

So, to all the dreamers of God's dreams... dream on!

**For the original, full version of The Joseph Chronicles, Level 1, check out Genesis chapter 37 verses 2 to 36 in the Bible.**

# LEVEL 2

# An X-cellent Dude

*When Kurt Cobain of Nirvana fame committed suicide, most the world's music press couldn't believe it.*

*Here was this talented young guy at the height of his creative powers, with all the benefits money and fame could buy. He had a pretty young wife and millions of fans the world over.*

*His death just didn't fit the picture. It was so unexpected. People who admired him from a distance had built a mental profile of Kurt. It obviously did not square with the reality of his life.*

For those who knew him well, however, Cobain's untimely end was not a total shock. They knew of his long battles with depression and drugs. They knew about his self-destructive tendencies. They knew he was fighting some heavy inner demons.

The tragedy is that guys like Kurt, who have so much talent and are worshipped from afar by so many, have to spend so much time and energy being 'cool' that they can't afford to be 'real'. While they're tending their carefully stage-managed images, their real lives are in turmoil and there's nothing anyone can do to help while the emotional walls are up.

## Not Cool, But Real!

The man who has influenced human history the most was not very cool at all. In fact, you might say that in some ways he was the most *uncool* guy the world has seen. Some of the things he taught seem downright weird at first thought.

He taught, for example, that we're most happy when we have deep-seated needs we know we can't fill (see Matthew 5:3). He said that real living is about laying down our own interests and rights to pursue much higher goals (see Mark 8:35). His teaching and his life ran against the grain of what the world calls 'cool'.

Yet he was the most *real* man in history! People who heard him talk said that he spoke as if he really knew what was what; as if he was connected to a higher authority than other religious teachers and philosophers (see Matthew 7:29).

On top of that, he worked miracles that were clearly not stage-managed conjuring tricks. He was transparent; he didn't hide behind clichés, or try to stay aloof from the gritty realities of people in need. He made himself available and went *looking* for people to help. He didn't cringe behind the niceties of political correctness; he took an open stand on issues, even when that cost him dearly.

His name, of course, was Jesus Christ.

It seems to me that the modern world's view of what is cool - what is worth imitating and admiring - is very distorted. We shrug off the things God calls important, dismissing them as impossible ideals or boring restrictions on our personal freedom.

It just might be, though, that if we spent less time trying to be cool, we might actually find the time to be *real* and to let God help us with the struggles we face. Having come to the end of the highway that leads to our own dreams, and finding there a desolate wasteland, we might start dreaming God's *better* dreams.

## Yesterday, All My Troubles Seemed So Far Away...

Remember our man Joseph? We left him dreaming big dreams, despite the stifling cynicism around him.

His brothers plotted his death because he held onto a vision of his future; a dream that he believed had come from God. Despite being surrounded by sceptics, he refused to let go of what he believed was a God-given sense of destiny. Even though he wasn't sure of the meaning of his strange night visions, he knew they called him to greatness. And he was prepared to stick with them until they eventually worked their way into reality.

In Level 2 of these Chronicles, we find young Joe somewhere in the bowels of Egypt, the world superpower of the day.

If you've travelled, you know the buzz that comes from touching down in some new port of call, especially if it's a huge city that's packed with attractions. But Joe's entry to Egypt is filled with anything *but* excitement.

Here he is, a teenager who's never been away from his small town home. Suddenly, he's thrust into a frightening foreign environment, not as a tourist, but as the property of a black market slave ring.

Joseph knows that even if he can somehow free himself and return home, his brothers will probably find another way to get rid of him. They may even kill him next time.

His mind is filled with questions: 'How will I get on with these slave merchants? Will they treat me well, or will they make my life unbearable? Will I be with them for long? Or does fate have something even worse in store for me?'

As it turns out, it's not long before he's sold into the house of an Egyptian government official, a guy named Potiphar. This man has money, power and a wife-to-kill-for. He immediately puts Joseph to work.

As days and months go by, thoughts of home and family fill Joseph's mind. Working the fields, he daydreams of minding sheep for his father. Alone in the servants' quarters at night, lying on his mat, he muses on what his brothers might be doing. They may have been cruel to him, but he misses them nevertheless.

As time passes in Potiphar's house, Joseph begins to notice something interesting. Even here in the house of a foreign master, stripped of his rights and freedoms, his work is very successful. Whatever he's working on, it seems to come out smelling like roses. It's as if everything he touches turns to gold. Someone up there is definitely smiling on him.

His boss is a sharp operator. He notices this gift of success. Potiphar thinks, 'Hey, this young guy from Shepherdsville really has something going for him - he's living under some kind of good cosmic vibe or something. Whatever it is, he's worth having around.' So, he sets Joseph apart for special treatment.

After only a short time at Potiphar Inc., Joseph is promoted to manager of the entire household. He's still a young man and he's still a slave, but at least he's a better *class* of slave now. He has a few basic freedoms. He can make decisions that will advance the master's cause. It's not much, but it's better than your basic grovel-in-the-dirt servitude.

Then, just when Joe's luck seems to be changing, he develops the worst kind of trouble - woman trouble.

Mrs. Potiphar, the boss' wife, has an eye for young male talent. A few years ago, she was crowned Miss Egypt. Ever since, she's been working to make sure she never loses her youthful figure and healthy skin. Potiphar has already forked out a fortune on aerobics classes, sunlamp sessions and mystical, oriental bath lotions.

She's only a few years older than Joseph and she's drop-dead gorgeous! Potiphar really knows how to pick 'em.

Early in her marriage, Mrs. P. had revelled in her socially prominent position. She enjoyed being the beautiful, status symbol wife of a big shot. She had wined and dined, cruised and schmoozed with the best of them. She had indulged her expensive tastes in fashion and her love of fine food. For a while, life had been one big party.

In more recent times, though, her husband is looking less and less like the knight-in-shining-armour she thought she married. These days, he looks more and more like the middle aged, middle-ranking servant of Pharaoh that he really is. He's lost his youthful fire and ambition. He has few prospects for advancement - and he doesn't seem to care.

So, frustrated and feeling that life is passing her by, she starts looking for adventure in other quarters. And her wandering, heavily painted Egyptian eye comes to rest on Joseph, the strapping young executive in charge of hubby's household.

Now, our man Joseph is not only gifted, he's also incredibly handsome. What's more, he has natural charm and an indefinable charisma that leaves people thinking, 'This guy's going somewhere in life - somewhere important.'

**Someone up there seems to be smiling on Joseph!**

Mrs. P. decides that she wants him, no matter what. He's the diversion she's been needing. He'll bring back a little spice and adventure into her dreary life. It's not too often that people refuse her. Besides he's a slave, so there isn't much he can say about it. He is hers for the taking.

She plots and plans. The timing has to be just right.

One day, Potiphar departs on yet another business trip, raking up the frequent-rider points on his camel. Later that afternoon, Joseph sits quietly in his room taking a well-earned break between jobs.

Dressed in ancient Egypt's version of a Gucci evening dress, Mrs. Potiphar slinks into his room, smiles seductively and gets right to the point of the exercise.

'Come to bed with me, honey, I want you,' she purrs. She's not one for romance, or 'Let's get to know each other.' With her, it's straight down to business.

## Tell Me What You Want, What You Really, Really Want...

Put yourself in Joseph's shoes for a minute.

The boss is away and his wife wants to play. An hour of pure pleasure awaits him.

It's obvious that this lady is very unhappy and bored with her husband. She's crying out for the attentions of a *real* man. *She* has needs, *he* has needs... so what could be simpler than using one another to meet those needs?

Besides, what does Joseph owe Potiphar? Nothing. He was born a free man and now he's a slave. Potiphar has snatched away his freedom. Potiphar keeps him from going home. Potiphar stands between him and all his dreams.

Everybody says that Joseph is the best thing that's happened to this house for a long time. Since he arrived they've enjoyed one success after another. People are even saying that the favour of God is on Joseph; that he has the touch of heaven on him.

Perhaps this is his chance to take a little back for himself. He deserves it. Now he can keep some of that 'heavenly favour' he's been splashing around so generously. He can take care of number one for a change.

But that isn't how Joseph responds.

## Go On - Surprise Me!

Success in life is not really about making one great decision *once* in your lifetime. It's about making many smaller, righteous decisions over a long period of time.

You are not simply the product of what others say about you, or the result of how circumstance has treated you. You are a product of how you choose to *respond* to life's challenges.

Your destiny is ultimately shaped by *you* - through the decisions that *you* make. Your power of choice is one of the greatest of all God's gifts to you, because it allows you to shape how your life turns out in the end.

Faced with the alluring Mrs. Potiphar, Joseph makes a choice that has to be one of the most difficult choices anyone *can* make. At a time when people have been taking everything *from* him, he chooses to respond in the opposite spirit. While others have acted toward him with a total disregard for his needs or desires, he decides to respond with a *generous* spirit.

Mrs. Potiphar has her arms around his neck and her lips are open to give him a killer kiss. 'I'm all yours babe,' she breathes. 'Do whatever you want with me...'

Joseph jumps back, nearly toppling her as she presses against him.

'Get off!' he shouts. 'How can I do this to my master? He has trusted me with everything in his house... except you, his wife? How can I abuse his trust, and offend God like this? Thanks, but no thanks!'

**You are a product of how you choose to respond to life's challenges.**

Think about it: it's a brave decision. What has Joseph done?

He's come to a turning point in his life. He has chosen to live with excellence.

## X-cellent!

True excellence is a generosity of spirit that pushes us beyond what is normal.

Jesus said that if we're going to be his followers, we must live in ways that constantly surprise people. We must do what is *not* expected. We must go *beyond* the average in the good things we do.

Jesus said that it's no real credit to us if we love those who love us, because even ungodly people do that. There's nothing special about giving money to those who can then return the favour - even unbelievers do that.

He said that we should love those who have no time for us and share our goods with people who can't give anything back. Then people will see that there's a higher compassion and a greater power motivating our actions (see Luke 6:32-35).

Someone has said, 'The greatest witness for Jesus is a life you can't explain unless there's a God.'

I believe that our world will take more notice of Christians when we live as if there really *is* a God in heaven. When we imitate his generous way of life. When we give beyond the norm and go the extra mile for others.

God is challenging his church today to mirror his excellence of spirit, in a world that's worn down by selfishness and impoverished through individualism.

Let's make this practical. How do we make a start at living with excellence? Let's begin with the measure Jesus used for finding a generous heart: our attitude to money.

A lot's been said about Christians and money. But what did Jesus say? What does the Bible *really* teach?

## Money, Bread, Mulla, Dosh

There are basically two groups at the extremes of Christian teaching on money:

### 1. The friends of St. Francis

Francis of Assisi was a young man of noble character who decided to give all of his wealth away and live among the poor. He taught his followers to do the same.

It was a laudable attitude and one that God blessed. But it's not necessarily a lifestyle that is the will of God for *all* Christians. Actually, the Bible is very clear that God wants us to be blessed so that we have enough to share with others in need. After all, how can the problem of poverty be solved by more poverty? (See Psalm 37:25-26.)

Some will say, 'Hey, Mother Teresa was poor, and look at the good she did!' Yes, but *was* this remarkable woman of God really without resources?

I think she actually understood the principle of God's blessing very well indeed. She constantly raised money from many quarters, always keeping her faith in God and not people. The money she raised enabled her to feed and clothe thousands of poor and sick people in Calcutta and throughout the world. She didn't wait until she had money before she did what the Lord commanded, but she definitely wasn't shy in asking for money in his name.

In many places, the Bible talks about God blessing his people so that they can *be* a blessing. Some of God's best friends in the Bible were quite wealthy people. In fact, it was his smile on their lives that *enabled* them to become rich (see Genesis 24:35).

> **Our world will take more notice of Christians when we give beyond the norm and go the extra mile for others.**

It's pretty hard to give when you have nothing. It's difficult to strive for God's *big* goals in your life if you're wondering where your next meal is coming from. It's impossible to use your faith for *great* things, if you need to use it believing for life's mundane things.

### 2. The God, gold and glory gang

These are the folks at the opposite end of the spectrum from St. Francis. They teach that if you don't have a big car and a fancy house you're not really a person of strong faith. They believe that you can measure people's faith by what they possess.

Jesus, however, warned us about the dangers of a money-hungry life. 'A man's real life,' he said, 'can't be measured by the things he possesses' (Luke 12:15). He also said, 'No one can serve two masters... You cannot serve both God and Money' (Luke 6:24). God has no problem with money, but he does have a problem with greed and with a materialistic lifestyle.

The Bible also clearly teaches that we should never judge people by externals, such as what they wear (see James 2:3-4).

## Money, Money, Money

So what does God want from me when it comes to money? Well, it's pretty simple really:

### a) God wants me to set limits for my life

Many Christians seem to have values that are little different from those of the consumerist world around them. Their attitude is, 'When the money's there I'll spend it and when it's gone, it's gone.'

But faith calls us to be more responsible than that. We each need to decide before God how much of our increase we will use for our own needs, and how much we will set aside to give: to God, to his church and to other people.

I can't set those limits for you and you can't set them for me. That would be Pharisaic. We must each sort out for ourselves, in good conscience and obedience to what God's word tells us, just where to draw the line for our own individual lifestyles.

*After all, there are only so many clothes you can wear, only so many CDs you can listen to and only so many houses you can live in.*

### b) God wants me to live adventurously

Have you ever bitten off more than you can chew, in response to a clear call from God? When did you last do something that people might look at and say, 'Either you're a fruitcake or there is a God'?

Faith is spelt R.I.S.K. You can't live for Jesus and play it safe all the time. Commit yourself to living for something bigger than you are, to using your energies and gifts to build the kingdom of God in this world and not your own little fiefdom. God honours that kind of living.

### c) God wants me to give dangerously

Hey, just about every Christian knows what Philippians 4:19 says: 'God will supply all your needs according to his riches in glory by Christ Jesus.' But not many bother to read the verses immediately before that.

Paul was writing these words to a group of Christians who had given to his mission out of their own need. They had given *sacrificially,* even when it meant they would not have much left over. To people like that God makes a special promise: 'You've met the needs of my work using your limited resources. Now, I'm going to meet all *your* needs using my *un*limited resources, through Christ.'

Money's not the only thing with which we need to be generous, but it's how we deal with money that highlights a generous spirit more than anything else. That's what Jesus meant when he said that you could tell where a person's heart is by where they put their money (see Matthew 6:21). If you're generous with finances, you'll be generous with other things too.

# Why Give?

Does God need my money? No, he owns everything anyway. Ultimately, everything people *think* they own is just on loan to them. So, why is giving so important? God wants me to learn to give because:

## 1. Giving releases control

God can't use anything in my life that I won't release completely to him. He wants me to surrender all of my life, with no strings attached.

When I give money in his name I am also releasing into his hands all that my money represents: the time, talent and energy it took for me to earn that money. The cash is just a token of all that is important to me. When I give money, I'm in effect releasing control of my time, my talent and my energy.

## 2. When I give he can bless me

God has built a principle of sowing and reaping into all of his creation. What - and how - you sow determines what - and how - you reap. What you receive in life is determined by how much, how wisely and with what attitude you give out. What's more, if God can trust you with a little, he will eventually allow you to oversee much more! (See Galatians 6: 9; 2 Corinthians 9:7-10.)

## 3. Giving is a God-like thing to do

This is the ultimate reason for doing *anything* in life: because it is what our Father in heaven is doing.

Jesus said that he was able to perform amazing miracles because he copied what the Father was doing (see John 5:19-20). He told his followers that his teaching was a reflection of what his Father said (see John 8:26).

Success as a Christian means copying God in as many areas of life as possible - in the strength and power that he alone can give.

At a time of great need in his life, Joseph decided to act with a giving spirit that pushed his actions beyond the norm. Throughout his life, this attitude always set him up for future success. Whatever was going on around him, Joseph maintained a generous attitude - with his resources, his gifts, his time and his forgiveness.

Even when it would have been easy for him to grasp things for himself - and to justify doing so - Joseph responded with generosity. This became the pattern for a life of excellence.

*For the original, full version of The Joseph Chronicles, Level 2, check out Genesis chapter 39 in the Bible.*

# LEVEL 3

# What Are Friends For?

*You are a product not so much of your environment,
or of what others do to you. You are primarily a product
of your own choices.*

*Even when people hurt you in the most terrible ways,
you have the ability, with God's help, to forgive them
and move on with your life.*

The story of Joseph showcases just how our own decisions can empower us to overcome tough times. In fact, as the saga of Joseph unfolds, we learn that negative events can be turned around: what was meant to do us harm can be used for our good, if we have the right attitude toward others and the correct heart towards God.

So far, young Joe has been sold by his brothers to a black market slave ring. He's served as a slave in the house of an Egyptian military officer. While there, he's proven himself a valuable and trustworthy worker.

Then a self-centred and vindictive woman wrongfully accuses him of rape. Just as things seem to be moving forward for him, he's accused of a crime and thrown - without a fair trial - into an Egyptian prison.

If this were me, I'd be pulling out the Muddy Waters albums about now. I'd be singing the blues and wallowing in the mud of self-pity. Strangely, though, even in that dark prison you can see Joseph's lucky star shining through.

After a few months in prison, the head guard starts to notice Joseph. During his career as head keeper, prisoners have come and gone by the hundreds. But this young guy seems a cut above the rest.

It's not his clothes, it's not his speech - in fact, it's hard to put your finger on exactly *what* it is. There's just some unique quality about him. It's as if he was born under a special star - and not even the dingy, crusty environment of a dungeon can kill the favour on his life.

It's not just good luck that sets him apart. After all, you could hardly call this kid lucky, in the normal sense of the word. There's nothing especially 'lucky' about being thrown into the king's prison for something you claim you didn't do. There's nothing 'lucky' about being sold into slavery in the first place.

No, it's something else that makes this guy special. Even when things are at their worst and others are sinking without trace, Joseph always seems to have his head above water.

So, fascinated by his positive attitude and drawn to his natural sense of hope, the prison warden takes Joseph under his wing. With Joe's already well-developed management skills, it's not long before he's got that prison ticking over like a reliable Swiss watch. He's a hard worker and he doesn't mind serving the needs of others - very rare qualities inside a jail!

I've visited people in prison a number of times. Each time I've gone into a prison, I've thought to myself, 'How would I be feeling right now if I knew I would not be coming out again tonight?' I've always been more than a little relieved to see the gates open wide for me on the way out.

There can be very few more terrifying experiences on earth than being forcibly cut off from the life you know and shut away behind walls and bars. Knowing that the world outside will be moving on without you. It must be one of the loneliest of all feelings. That's why Jesus told us to visit prisoners: to show that they're *not* forgotten and that *God* hasn't given up on them (see Matthew 25:36-40).

Though most of us, thankfully, do not have to endure anything like prison life, we've all had times when we've felt isolated, forgotten and alone. You know, those times when you feel as if there are *invisible* bars all around you. Those times when you've been mistreated and misunderstood and you feel you couldn't *be* more forgotten - even if you were dead. Those times when you ask, 'What on God's earth is happening to me?'

## Why Me?

The first question we ask when things seem to fold in around us is 'Why?' What we really mean, of course, is 'Why me?'

Tough times can arise in our lives for any of five major reasons.

## 1. Sin

First of all, tough times often occur because of what the Bible calls 'sin'. The word comes from an old English expression that was used when an archer aimed at a target and fell short.

That's what sin is - not just the breaking of some rules, but a moral falling short. Sin means missing God's standard and purpose for our lives. Sin is an abuse of our God-given right to make choices.

If I make choices that fit in with God's ways I will overall enjoy a life of blessing. If I make decisions that constantly fall short of the good and right things for which God has designed

**All sin is a form of insanity and self-destruction.**

me, I am setting myself against the moral laws that govern the universe.

In the end, all sin is a form of insanity and self-destruction. When I continually choose what is less than God's best for me I will find myself heading full-speed down dangerous, dead-end streets.

## 2. Righteousness

A second reason we go through tough times has to do with *righteousness* - the very opposite of sin. There will be times when I'm doing what is *right,* making *good* choices and things will still go wrong around me. Why?

It's partly because people often prefer darkness to light. The Bible says that many people will move deeper into darkness when light appears - to keep their wrong deeds, thoughts and attitudes from being exposed (see John 3:20-21).

We have all done, said, or thought things of which we are later ashamed. We'd hate for those things to be brought out into the light of day, to have the world see our dirty washing.

Without the cleansing power of Jesus working on the inside of us, we're all drawn to the darkness, even while our heart is yearning for the light.

So, it's not surprising that people feel threatened by anyone who is able to break with the darkness and walk freely in the light. If you're just going along with the crowd you make others feel satisfied with their mistakes - even if, deep down, they *know* they were born for better things.

Once you start bucking the system, though, once you start living as if there's a better alternative, people start to feel uncomfortable. Some of them will try to pull you back, rather than join you. You make them feel guilty; you show them what they *could be* and they're not sure they want to know. As soon as you start marching to a different drum, you become a needle prodding at their conscience.

The Bible actually promises that anyone who wants to live a godly life will suffer persecution of one form or another (see Mark 10:29-30). If people around you are choosing to hide their deeds in darkness, they're not going to feel too good about anyone who turns on the light.

### 3. A fallen world

Sometimes we go through prison house experiences just because we live in a fallen world.

The world in which we live is beautiful, to be sure. The colours, the sounds, the textures - the size, the power, the energy - the whole thing is incredible! Sometimes, when you really just stop to take it in, it just takes your breath away.

That's why the Bible says that the natural creation tells us so much about God and what he's like (see Romans 1:20).

As spectacular as it is, though, this amazing world is not the way God first designed it to be. In Eden's garden, there was no air or noise pollution, no ozone-depleting chemical waste, no endangered species. It was a place of perfect peace and inno-cence and complete tranquillity. No lie had ever stolen in to destroy the peace; no voice had ever been raised in fury; no angry shot had ever been fired in war.

There was no need for that to change. Nothing God had programmed into his creation was designed to destroy the harmony in this symphony of stillness and calm.

It was human rebellion that brought the curtain down. Since that far-off time, human sin has introduced a malignant corrup-tion into the world, a persistent twisting of things away from the will of God.

We pay a high price for our sinfulness. Things keep winding down and heading toward the lowest common denominator, not only in our natural environment, but in our thoughts and actions and in our relationships too. And terribly unfair things sometimes happen to the nicest and most upstanding people.

Ours is a fallen world. It's a broken world that's waiting to be mended (see Romans 8:19-22). Sometimes, we have negative experiences simply because we're living in a fallen world.

### 4. Devil's work

According to the Bible, there is a malevolent spiritual being in this world who is out to destroy every good thing God has ever made - including you and me. The Bible gives him several names, but the most well known today is 'Satan', which means 'accuser'.

Satan's nature is totally perverted by pride and rebellion against God. Driven by an insane jealousy of humanity, whom God loves so much, Satan is bent on our destruction. Oh, he doesn't mind if you and I just cruise through life from cradle to grave and never give him another thought. In fact, it makes his job a whole lot easier if people think he doesn't exist, if people pay him no attention at all.

However, if you start to work *against* his kingdom of darkness, if you really start to get a hold of God's plan for your life... well, he can get awfully cranky. He's very good at throwing stuff at you: from the mud of innuendo, to the sticks and stones of biting criticism, to the fire-tipped arrows of accusations and the crippling landmines of sickness and disease.

Thankfully, if you're a Christian, you know that the Jesus you serve has already *defeated* Satan on the cross; that Satan has no more power over you; that his attacks can be faced *and overcome* in the power and protection of God's Holy Spirit; that you only have to call out the name of Jesus to find deliverance, cleansing and hope. (See Colossians 2:15; 1 Corinthians 15:57; Romans 8:37, 10:13, 16:20; Ephesians 6:11-18.)

## God Stretches Us (Ouch!)

Hang on a minute... Didn't I say that there were *five* reasons for the tough times we face? What's the fifth one?

Sometimes our difficult times are caused not by Satan's work - though he'll use *any* situation to his advantage, if we let him. Some of our uncomfortable experiences are the result of *God's* dealings and discipline in our lives. The Bible says that, rather than complaining about God's discipline we should be grateful for it. He only disciplines those who are truly his children, those he treats as sons (see Hebrews 12:5-7). God's discipline in the here-and-now saves us from a future where we are judged and found wanting along with unbelievers (see 1 Corinthians 11:32).

When Jesus was facing the agony of imminent crucifixion, he didn't say, 'Satan, get behind me!' as he did on another occasion. He said, 'Father... not my will but yours be done' (Luke 22:42). He recognized that the cross would not be the work of Satan, but the plan and purpose of God.

Though we will never have to go through the experience Jesus went through for us, there are times when we too will find that God is shaping us for something bigger, in sometimes painful ways.

In Mark 8:34, Jesus said that we must take up our cross and follow him. Notice: we're not told to take up *his* cross, because *he* has taken that particular pain *for us*. Thank God, we will never have to go through the spiritual agony Jesus endured on that Roman torture stick.

**There are times when we will find that God is shaping us for something bigger.**

We'll never have to feel that God has abandoned us; that he has turned away in anger, unable to look upon our sin any longer. That particular cross will never be ours.

We must take up *our* cross. We must follow Jesus' example by dying to all the old values, habits and priorities that governed our lives before we met him. Now that we've made him Lord of our lives, he must be the guiding factor in all our plans. He must be the model for our lives; the ideal standard for which we'll aim in all of our behaviour.

Sadly, many Christians have a 'near death experience'. They never quite die to self. Jesus taught that unless a seed falls into the ground and dies, it can never reproduce itself and it remains alone. But when it dies, it brings forth great quantities of fruit (see John 12:24). The secret to gaining a successful and increasingly influential life is death to self. We must die to our old ways so that we can live unto God and his higher ways (see John 12:25-26).

# A Positive Result

Someone who doesn't know the Lord might ask, 'If God takes you through tough times, what's the difference between his works and those of Satan?'

There's a very big difference: God's work produces more *good* in us; it always ends in greater righteousness and peace. Satan's work only ever brings pain and spiritual destruction and robs us of our destiny under God (see John 10:10).

The trying times God takes us through always produce very positive results - if we stay humble and soft in his hands. For one thing, they develop *character* in us (see James 1:3-4). Godly trials produce maturity, if we let them.

They also *reveal* our character. Trials bring out what is *already in us;* they show God, us and other people what his work has already produced. They prove the quality of our inner life and the strength of our call; they show just how much God has done in our lives.

When our character is matured and proven, we come to a new level of spiritual and moral authority.

When Mother Teresa died, many people in the media shared the experiences they'd had with her. One prominent TV reporter said, 'Whenever Mother Teresa asked me to do something, I just couldn't say no. I felt like I was in the presence of a higher moral authority.' This wonderful woman of God had authority *because* her character and her call had been tested and proven so many times.

God also uses tough times to refocus our priorities. When the lights go out in a room, the first thing you do is start feeling around, to find out where you are in relation to your surroundings. When shadows seem to creep across life's path, we re-think what's important to us - and what's important to God - and we re-establish where we are in relation to him.

God's tough times also have a way of building a new anticipation in us. Our spiritual temperature, the level of our faith, starts rising. As our faith rises, we find that we can believe God for bigger things. We start looking for a much larger future in him.

Yes, even the most committed Christians, the people of strongest faith, will sometimes feel like they've been through a cement mixer backwards! In the end, though, those difficult experiences can stretch our capacities, enlarge our faith, give us a stronger resolve to run our race *and* inspire a deeper hunger for more of God.

## Nobody Knows The Trouble I've Seen...

Now, back to Joseph.

He's still in the prison. There's no way he can understand what's happening in his life. He's just got to trust that God knows what he's doing.

One particular day, he's sitting alone in his cell when the door swings open to admit two new inmates. After some quick introductions all round, the men begin to tell the stories of how they came to be here.

Each of them was at one time a personal servant and advisor to Pharaoh, the king of all Egypt. Both had great prestige and status and a huge pay packet.

Somehow they have both fallen out of favour with the king. They're not too open at this point, as if they're embarrassed to give details. Each of them says he could have been hung for his crime, so it must have been something significant.

Over the next few weeks, Joseph gradually gets to know them a little. He enjoys talking with these men who've had experience in the royal house. Besides, he still hasn't forgotten his dreams of a lofty and influential position, though he still doesn't completely understand what they mean - and he certainly can't see how they can come to pass while he's in prison.

One morning, he finds both of the king's former servants looking decidedly miserable - that is, more miserable than usual.

'What's up?' he says. 'You look like you've just been gargling with razor blades!'

'We've each had a dream,' they reply. 'We know the dreams mean something about our individual futures. But we can't interpret them and it's driving us crazy!'

Now Joseph is on turf that he knows well: dreams and visions. He's had the one great dream since he was a teenager.

Just then, sitting in that dark prison house, Joseph is faced with another major decision, one no less important than the choice he made in Potiphar's house. His options are clear: 'In this place of pain, loneliness, disappointment, and misunderstanding do I become hardened to the cries of these men, do I sink into self-pity, or do I invest what little I have in others?'

If he wants, Joseph can simply ignore the misery of these men. After all, what does he owe them? Nothing. At least they've *had* their moment in the sun, serving in the courts of Pharaoh. They've had their fifteen minutes of fame. Joe, on the other hand, has been abused, accused and misused for years. They should be helping *him*, not the other way around.

Or, he could take this opportunity to expound on his own dream. 'You call *that* a dream?' he could say. 'Let me tell you about a *real* dream!'

Here again, we see the quality of Joseph's heart shining through. Instead of dismissing these men, or bragging about his own dreams, Joseph makes the decision to become a mentor, to invest in the dreams of others.

**Even the most committed Christians sometimes feel like they've been through a cement mixer backwards!**

This is a choice you will face too. It will come when you least feel like facing it, when you probably feel that you have nothing more to give. Even in your own weakness, God will call you to invest in the development of someone else.

A mentor is simply someone who sees potential in another, less experienced person and invests time and energy to release their ability. To be a good mentor, you will need the following qualities:

### a) Grace
You will need to change in the other person only what God wants changed, in the way that *he* wants to do it. You will need to avoid being a control freak or a manipulator of others. You will need to decide what is really important and what is not, what needs to change and what does not, and leave the trivial issues alone.

### b) Sincerity
You will need to be *real up close*, to be able to say 'do as I do', not just 'do as I say'. People of this Millennial Generation need heroes they can touch. So many of the heroes our culture offers us are nothing more than fantasy figures from the world of celluloid

and videotape. They're not real; you can't get close enough to see their values at work in the gritty realities of daily life.

### c) Patience

When you first start trying to develop or teach someone else, you often need to look for them doing things *approximately* right. They won't get things completely right the first time and sometimes not even on the second or third attempt. You need to stick with it until they do get it right, giving encouragement and correction along the way.

**You will need to be able to say ´do as I do´, not just ´do as I say´.**

### d) Resourcefulness

You will need to be a sharer of resources, to provide your protégé with books, CDs, websites and other resources that will help them grow. You'll need to suggest seminars or other events they may want to attend.

You will need to share some of your personal relationships with them, exposing them to others who can develop their skills. And you'll need to accept that they won't learn everything they need to know from you alone. You can't feel threatened when they learn from others too.

### e) Loyalty

You will need to stand up for your protégé in public, even when they've done something wrong or made a mistake. They will need you to show that you're not ashamed of being on their side when the chips are down.

### f) Empathy

You'll certainly need to learn how to empathise with your friend - to hear not just the words they say, but to be very open and sensitive to the feelings behind those words. Sometimes, they'll just need for you to listen; at other times they'll need for you to challenge them to think in a different way.

### g) A releasing attitude

You will need to know when it's time to let go; when you need to release your protégé and watch them go on to other pastures. Their relationship to you will change. They may not seem to need you as much as they did before. Remember: though others will come along and influence them, people *never* really forget who their parents were!

Joseph could have settled for self-pity and self-indulgence, but he chose to make a mentoring investment in others. What will you choose when the going gets tough, when you don't quite understand what's going on around you?

**For the original, full version of The Joseph Chronicles, Level 3, check out Genesis chapter 40 in the Bible.**

# LEVEL 4

# Seize The Day!

*So, we come to level 4, the climax of these Chronicles. So far, Joseph has been sold into black market slavery by his spiteful and jealous brothers. He's been vilified by a master whom he served with nothing but loyalty and integrity.*

*He's been imprisoned on a trumped-up charge, the result of bitterness and vanity in the heart of a woman scorned. And he has worked for years in a dark dungeon somewhere in the bowels of Egypt's legal complex, out of sight and out of mind, while life slowly passes him by.*

Once upon a time - it seems a lifetime ago - Joseph had great dreams, huge visions of what he was going to accomplish with his life. Now those dreams are just a memory, sometimes pleasant and sometimes taunting. It seems there's no longer any hope that they will become a reality - not in this harsh, unforgiving world.

Yet, despite all the setbacks life has thrown at him, Joseph has maintained a consistent commitment to making right choices. Those choices, made in the toughest and darkest moments, have kept his heart pure. They have always caused him to move up a level whenever things looked at their most hopeless.

In Level 4 of these chronicles, we find him still languishing in his prison cell. It is from here that he makes his final great decision - and the one that ultimately leads him to his place of prominence, the land of his youthful dreams.

## So Many Choices...

Before we look at what that decision involves, we need to note again that each good choice Joseph made was built on an earlier choice.

He didn't just wake up one morning, find himself with some problems and make the one big decision that gave him his 'big break' and hurled him to fame, glory and prominence. No, Joseph made good decisions many times over.

Sometimes, he must have wondered if anyone would ever know he'd made those choices.

There'll be times when you feel that way, too. But God *is* watching, even when men have turned their backs on us. He will always honour in the open, those who make right and godly choices in the hidden place, where it's hardest (see Matthew 6:6).

## The Big One...

So, what *was* Joseph's final decision, his big move?

In the final chapter of these Chronicles, Joseph has been Pharaoh's 'guest' in the 'house of correction' for two long years.

> **God will always honour in the open, those who make right and godly choices in the hidden place.**

He knows every bit of graffiti on those prison walls and has probably added a few lines himself. He's grown used to prison food - even though back in his father's house, the *dog* would have eaten better.

Now he's feeling *completely* forgotten, even by those he's tried to help along the way.

He remembers a fellow prisoner, a former courtier to the king, who once came to him with a troubling dream. Rather than shrug him off, Joseph had invested time and compassion in interpreting the man's vision.

Joseph told him that even though things looked bleak just then, it wouldn't be long before he'd be released from prison and then restored to his position of favour in the royal house. His encouragement and his prophetic words had given this guy new hope, something positive to hang on to.

Not long after that, the man had been acquitted, forgiven and restored to his influential position, just as Joseph had predicted. But did he remember Joseph's kindness? Did he put in a kind word for Joseph with the authorities? No sir. He just looked after number one and got on with his life.

So, Joseph is alone - again. It seems that heaven is closing over him - again. Looks like the good guy finishes last - again.

God may seem a long way from that prison cell, but he *is* at work!

# Dream On...

Pharaoh, the so-called 'god-king' of Egypt and all its vast territories, has two strange and deeply affecting dreams. Pharaohs in these times are always having dreams. In itself, that is not so surprising or unusual. It happens all the time...

For Joseph's contemporaries, dreams are portents of what is to come. They don't do the Freudian thing with dreams. They don't interpret their dreams as signs of repressed urges and submerged sexual drives. Dreams are not signals about the past at all - they are signposts to the future.

Pharaoh is king and he has great power, but nobody expects him to be a dream-reader. He has a special task force for that. His sages and soothsayers are on hand day and night to interpret anything he wants. So, he dials 'S' for 'seer' and tells them his dream.

'Can you translate this vision and tell me what it means?' the king asks, with just a hint of a threat in his tone.

'Oh yes, great king,' they respond, nervously. 'It's a tough one, that's for sure. But we have special ways of deciphering these riddles. We'll get right on it.'

So, off they go. They get out their tea leaves, they read the giblets of dogs and they refer to their astrological charts. Sadly, while they've been able to get by with all that in the past, they just can't seem to crack the code this time. They can't come up with a satisfactory interpretation of the king's dreams.

Meanwhile, Pharaoh is walking around like he's had a three-day visit to the dentist. He's irritable and angry - and that spells danger for everyone around him.

# Remember Me?

One of Pharaoh's household advisors starts thinking back on his stint in the local prison house. He figures that if things continue as they are, Pharaoh might well put him right back in there!

Suddenly, he recalls a young Hebrew who was kind to him, a young guy who seemed to be able to give accurate (and positive) interpretations for dreams. Perhaps this guy could help the king...

Finally, someone remembers Joseph!

At times, *you* may feel as Joseph did, forgotten and

overlooked. But you can be sure of one thing. Nothing you will ever do for God - even in secret, *especially* in secret - is ever forgotten or overlooked by him. He will *always* reward in the open the good you do in private, no matter how small or seemingly insignificant.

Why? Because he is a *just* God. He always ensures that the truth comes out, one way or the other. God will not allow you to be ignored forever, if your heart is right toward him.

> **Nothing you do for God is ever forgotten or overlooked by him.**

In all his ups and downs, Joseph has never once allowed bitterness or negativity to take a firm hold in his heart. He's kept an attitude of faith in God, even when his faith in man has been shaken to the core.

'Oh great king, live forever,' says the servant, as he creeps into the king's chamber, bowing low. 'I think I may have come up with a solution to your dream problem.'

'You see, there's this guy I know who's really good with dreams, especially tough ones. I'm sure he'd be able help, oh great one. The only problem is, he's in your prison...'

'Well, don't just stand there, you fool,' shouts Pharaoh. 'Get him in here! *Now!*'

So, after a shave and a haircut, Joseph is ushered into the presence of Egypt's king. The palace is dazzling and more than a bit overwhelming for someone who's been in prison for years.

After the first nerve-wracking moments when he's introduced to Pharaoh, Joseph humbly and patiently listens as the king spills his dreams.

'They're certainly weird dreams,' Joseph says to himself. 'But, hey, being an all-powerful Pharaoh is probably prone to leave you a little on the crazy side.'

'Anyway, God often speaks in unusual ways, just to get our attention! I know he has a purpose in this situation.'

And this is Joseph's crowning moment. This is where he makes his final great decision, the choice that once-and-for-all seals his destiny and opens the way for his God-given dream to come true.

Joseph makes the momentous decision to *seize the day*.

He suddenly sees it clearly: *everything God has taken him through has been a preparation for this particular day.*

God has brought him to the point where he can step into the role for which he was born.

It's sad to see so many people - even Christians - living only for what they're trained for, and never finding out what they were born for! What you're trained for may be your career, but what you're born for is your *calling*.

God will shape circumstances and events and he will speak to you through his word, through prophecies and through the good advice of godly friends. He will go to great lengths to lead you to the point where you can launch out into *your* season of real significance.

Face it: life is short. You're born, you live and then one day you die. But the bit in the middle is what's important - and it's up to you what you make of it.

Will you follow God's call upon your life, will you let him mould you into shape and train you for the great project and ministry he's created for you? Or, will you wander in ever decreasing circles, avoiding at all costs any hint of sacrifice?

Will you make the commitment to living a life of patient, determined faith, or will you do what so many others in your generation are doing - looking for the quick-fix solution, waiting for the 'big break' that will make them great?

## It All Comes Down To This...

Joseph's big moment has arrived; God has set it up.

But even now he is required to take an initiative, to be *pro*active rather than just *re*active. Pushing boldly forward with his faith in the God who brought him here, he takes the biggest risk of his life.

'King, the bottom line in your dreams is this,' he says. 'There's going to be seven years of plenty throughout the land of Egypt. After that, there will be seven years of severe drought and famine.'

'What you need to do is this...' Now, he's really getting bold. 'You need to appoint a wise and trustworthy man to go throughout the land and collect a food tax during the next seven years.'

'Under his leadership, a percentage of everyone's crops should be stored away in the king's silos for the hard times to come. That's what your dream was telling you, and that's how we should respond.'

There it is... he's said it. The air in the throne-room is tense. Joseph's fate is in God's hands now. Will Pharaoh accept his counsel and pardon his audacity? Or will he throw him back on the refuse pile in prison?

To everyone's relief, Pharaoh starts to smile. It's not one of his vindictive, 'off-with-his-head' smiles. It's a beaming smile of approval, even surprise.

> **What you're trained for may be your career, but what you're born for is your calling.**

'That is truly amazing!' exclaims the king. He looks around at his courtiers. 'Where have you been hiding this guy all these years?'

He turns again to look down on Joseph.

'I'll tell you one thing, young man. After what I've seen and heard today, there's not a person in my entire kingdom who's more qualified for the position you describe than you are.'

'What was your name again? Joseph? I'm going to give you all the authority you'll need to get the job done.'

'You will speak with the complete backing of Pharaoh. I'm giving you total authority to represent me throughout my entire kingdom.'

So, in one day, Joseph is snatched from prison and made a senior advisor to Pharaoh! Not a bad day...

## A Huge Risk!

Remember, though: there's a huge risk for Joseph here. Think about it...

With most of the prophecies we hear in the church today, be they private or public, we can pretty much judge whether they're accurate when they're first given.

If you receive a prophetic word, you can usually measure it against the circumstances you're in at the time. You can also line it up against how God has led you in the past. You can say, 'Yes, that sounds like what God has been telling me,' or, 'No, that's so far off base it might apply to someone on Mars!'

Joseph's prophecy is way out *past* left field! He makes bold statements, knowing that he'll have an incredible *seven years* to ponder whether he's right or wrong!

There'll be seven years of plenty in the land and everyday he'll be quietly thinking the same thing: 'Did I get it right? What if there *is* no food shortage after this? What will people do to me? I've spent seven years taxing them to cover the famine. What if it doesn't come? They'll kill me!'

Many people wait for God to speak in a way that will call for zero risk on their part. A true word from God will always - *always* - involve risk. Remember, faith is spelt R.I.S.K. and the Bible says, 'without faith it is impossible to please God...' (Hebrews 11:6).

Oral Roberts, the great healing evangelist, has said: 'Faith is living on the edge of insecurity!'

Johann Wolfgang Von Goethe wrote: 'The right man is the one who seizes the moment.'

God is looking for that right man or woman, the one who will step out of the boat on the strength of nothing more than a command from heaven. Someone who will seek no more security than the knowledge that God has spoken, because that's enough.

At a British leadership conference a few years ago, I was asked to speak on this question: 'If you had 15 minutes left to live what would you say to these people?'

I thought long and hard about it. I'd like to leave you with my responses, because they line up exactly with Joseph's attitude. They will help you understand what it means to 'seize the day'.

## 1. Do something!
Many Christians are praying for a revelation that God has already given.

Jesus already told us what our life's work is to be, in broad terms: 'Go into all the world and preach the gospel and make disciples in my name...' (see Mark 16:15; Matthew 28:18).

Where is the will of God for you right now? Well, I know one thing. It doesn't start in some big arena somewhere, with you occupying centre stage, doing your thing under the spotlight. The will of God for your life starts in your school or college; in the local hospital; in the old folks' home. In short, wherever there is human need that you have the resources to meet.

Everything God gives you is in part for someone else. So, success in life begins with simply finding a need and meeting it - in Jesus' name, on his behalf and in the ability that he gives.

## 2. Do something prophetic

People today don't want more talk - they want action and experience.

If I showed you a photo of my family, you might say, 'Hey, great family...' They *are* a great family, but you could never really know my wife Davina, or Deanna, Grant and Jade from that photo. To know them you would have to interact with them in a personal way. A photo is just a representation, an image frozen in the past. What you need is a *manifestation*, the present reality.

For years, the Western church has given people nothing more than photos of God - representations of him: in theology, ritual and tradition. We have given people images of God frozen in time; pictures of what he did twenty or fifty years (if not centuries) ago.

Now, God doesn't change - ever. So, it is right and proper to point people back to what God did in the past. That's what the Bible is for: to help us learn what God is like through his dealings with people in the past (see 1 Corinthians 10:11). But the Bible story is given so that people can apply the lessons of the past to the *here and now*!

God knows that what people want and need most is a here-and-now manifestation of his power, his love and his presence. People *need* to see the gifts (or 'manifestations') of the Holy Spirit spoken of in 1 Corinthians 12 and 14. People *need* to hear accurate prophecies and see the gifts of healings at work (see 1 Corinthians 14:23-25). People *need* to experience the signs and wonders that follow the preaching of God's word, backing it up (see Acts 14:3).

Doing something prophetic means two things. Firstly, it means to do something that people say can't be done - bringing God into places and situations where people don't expect to find him. It means to break down the walls of predictability.

Secondly, it means to do that something in the *power* of God, something you couldn't do on your own. That shows that God is more than a 'nice old guy in the sky'; that he *does* care about and interact with people in the real world.

## 3. Do something prophetic with passion

When you know God wants you to be involved in something, give it everything you've got!

Do as Jesus said: 'Love the Lord your God with all your heart and with all your soul and with all your mind and with all your strength [energy]' (Mark 12:30).

So many people today say they're not interested in God, simply because they think he's not interested in them. The God of the Bible is a *passionate* person! Look at Jesus: he knew how to be angry, how to be moved with compassion, how to weep, and how to laugh. (See John 2:15-17; Matthew 9:36; John 11:35; Luke 1:14.)

Jesus was passionate in *everything* he did - without ever being gushing, sentimental or out of control. That's part of what attracted people to him.

**Whatever you try to do for God, give it all you've got.**

Whatever you try to do for God, give it all you've got. Often, it's only when you reach your *extremity* that the power of God really kicks in.

## Think Back...

Let's take a minute just to look back over the life and times of Joseph the dream-chaser.

In his early days, he starts out as 'that dreamer', the boy his brothers love to hate. He becomes 'that Hebrew slave', the young man who refuses to lower his standards even for a beautiful woman and is targeted as a result.

Then Joseph becomes a prisoner, forgotten and alone, with only his faith in God and his dreams to keep him going. Though he invests himself unselfishly in others, they always seem to forget him in the end.

But that's not how the story ends, is it? In the final chapter of this amazing true story, Joseph is mixing with royalty. He's travelling throughout the land, first-class, with all expenses paid. He's having influence over whole nations with the full backing of Pharaoh. He's saving a generation from starvation and destruction.

All along, Joseph has made right decisions in the toughest of times. Sometimes only God has been around to see the choices he's made, but that is the one thing that has ultimately ensured his success.

Joseph didn't get to his position of ultimate influence just because he made good choices...

...He got there because *God saw him make those good choices!*

In spite of his youthful dreams, Joseph could *never* have foreseen where God wanted to take him.

Even when he was a boy working in his father's house, God was preparing him for Pharaoh's house.

Even when he laboured away so faithfully in Potiphar's house, God was building him to take on Pharaoh's house.

Even when he was struggling to keep his faith in the prison house, God was getting him ready for Pharaoh's house.

Everything in his journey was set up by God to position his character, skills and attitudes for his moment of ultimate significance - that one time when the total impact of his experiences would cause him to influence history.

**If you remain faithful, God will open a ´Pharaoh´s house´ to you.**

*God has a Pharaoh's house for you too.* It's a place of ultimate significance where everything he's ever led you  through will be woven together into one great design.

You may right now be in 'father's house'. You are learning to dream God's dream for your life and to keep the faith no matter what cynicism surrounds you. You are being formed and equipped for your future.

Perhaps you feel like you're in Potiphar's house. Here, you're proving yourself while serving someone else's vision. You're working hard to produce Potiphar's dream because you know that this kind of submission is a vital part of your preparation. You sense that you're not ready yet for the full vision God has in store for you.

Or, you may be in a prison house experience right now. You've been doing your best and trying to let God work his plan in your life. You have tried to do the right thing, even under extreme pressure. Suddenly, it seems like all the lights in your life have gone out at once. You feel forgotten and alone, as if nobody really comprehends how much you've put in, how much you've given of yourself.

The lesson of Joseph's life is this: if you remain faithful and try to walk close to the Lord even through the prison experiences, God will open a 'Pharaoh's house' to you - a place where you will influence people and situations on a scale you never would have thought possible.

# The Bottom Line

In the lives of great people, it is often possible to find some statement or series of statements that really sums up their values and the reason for their greatness.

That's true in Joseph's case. There's at least one key statement that really reveals the heart of the man. It gives us a clue as to why he could survive heartbreak and disappointment *and* turn it to greatness.

It's near the end of his epic story. He has finally revealed himself to his long-lost brothers. These siblings who hated him so much in the beginning, who sold him as a slave and told their father he'd been torn apart by wild animals.

Yes, there have been times through the years in Egypt when Joseph felt nothing short of vengeful rage toward them. Many times, he has had to deal with the anger in his heart, seeking God's help to forgive.

Sitting now in his opulent palace, surrounded by the trappings of power and prestige, it would be easy for Joseph to vent his anger, to take his revenge. Once again, though, he exercises his sovereign power of choice.

He turns to his brothers and says, 'Come close to me... I am your brother Joseph, the one you sold into Egypt!'

'And now, do not be distressed and do not be angry with yourselves for selling me here, because it was to save lives that God sent me ahead of you... God sent me ahead of you to preserve for you a remnant on earth and to save your lives by a great deliverance' (Genesis 45:4, 5, 7).

This must be one of the most beautiful statements in the Bible - a book that's filled with beautiful statements! This one statement sums up the whole of Joseph's greatness. Right to the end, he just kept making great choices.

Joseph refused to give anyone but God the right to decide what he would become. He chose to see *everything* - even his toughest challenges - as being in God's safe hands, a part of God's ultimate purpose for his life.

He refused to be robbed of God's calling on his life, which he recognised wasn't given just for his sake, but for the salvation of many other people. He simply would not exchange God's purpose for anything less noble.

# The Finish Line...

Why did I write this little book?

To encourage and inspire you.

To show you that today's problems don't have to decide tomorrow's destiny.

To help you pluck up the courage to make choices that are right, even when nobody but God sees.

To show you that, because God sees, he *will* honour decisions of excellence.

God *will* bring you through father's house, through Potiphar's house, through the prison house, to your Pharaoh's house.

It may take time, but you *will* get there, if you stay with the program and don't give up (see Galatians 6:9).

So, whatever you're facing right now, keep making good, God-pleasing choices...

See you in Pharaoh's House!

**For the original, full version of The Joseph Chronicles, Level 4, check out Genesis chapter 41 in the Bible.**

# ABOUT THE AUTHOR

*Mal Fletcher is committed to one thing above all else: making God famous!*

Mal is a respected Christian pioneer and leader, a TV producer and presenter and an internationally acclaimed speaker. In his unique and challenging style, he is explaining the Christian message to secular cultures via the media, outreach events and training conferences around the world. He is also equipping church leaders to relate the gospel to contemporary cultures.

His TV program, *EDGES with Mal Fletcher,* can now be seen in over 210 countries, on Christian and major secular networks. EDGES is a colourful, fast-paced TV program that takes a very different look at the social issues shaping the values of today's world and the lifestyles of tomorrow. It offers a Christian response to major social, moral and lifestyle issues. Issues covered include: terrorism, euthanasia, civil disobedience, robotics, witchcraft and more. These programs are breaking new ground by bridging the gap between Christian production and secular broadcasters. The programs also have a growing audience online at www.edges.tv.

Mal is the founder and executive director of *Next Wave International*™, a mission to the contemporary cultures of Europe. Through this rapidly expanding mission, he and his team are not only reaching the unchurched via city-wide events, the Internet, TV and more; they are also equipping church and business leaders in the skills of contemporary leadership. The *Master Classes* on communication, generations and leadership attract leaders from several nations.

Mal also is the pioneer and leader of the *Strategic Leadership Consultation* and *EYE* leadership networks across Europe. These annual network meetings bring together two generations of key apostolic Christian leaders in Europe for strategic planning and prayer. They have become 'must-attend' meetings for many of Europe's most successful church network leaders.

Mal's books have been translated into several languages and his articles feature regularly in major Christian publications. The Next Wave International™ websites attract thousands of visitors from around the world every month.

Originally from Australia, Mal is known in many nations as a pioneer leader and for his unique ability to communicate Christian truth in a thought-provoking, insightful and often humorous way that relates to secular and Christian audiences alike.

Mal was raised in a Christian home, and studied architecture in his home city of Melbourne before feeling a call to full time ministry in the early 1980s. Throughout the 80s and early 90s, he was the key pioneer of *Youth Alive Australia* and its first National Director. This exciting movement grew from just 300 young people to over 60,000 in 10 years, as the Spirit of God moved among that nation's youth and churches. It continues to grow and its model is now influencing many nations for Jesus.

Mal also pioneered a church in one of his country's leading new age and occult areas. His books on culture and leadership issues are now available in several languages.

Today, as well as heading up the mission to Europe and working in the media, Mal travels the world extensively teaching and preaching at leadership conferences and events. He has been married to Davina for more than twenty years and they have three children.

Information on Mal's personal appearances, plus photos, articles, audio files and books can be found at: **www.nextwaveonline.com**.

So, you've enjoyed reading this book?
Check out these other great resources from

# MAL FLETCHER

### at www.nextwaveonline.com

## DAILY RECHARGE
- **Bible-based daily devotions for every day of the year...** Mal's words will inspire and challenge you, and lift your faith to new levels.
- **You can also have it delivered daily to your PDA!**

## BOOKS
- **Making God Famous**
- **The Pioneer Spirit**
- **Burning Questions**

## E-BOOKS
- **GET REAL!**
- **The Joseph Chronicles**
- **Youth: The Endangered Species**

## AUDIO FILES & CDs
- **The Pioneer Spirit**
- **The Revival of Passion (9/11/2001)**
- **Winning the Battle for Influence**
- And many more of Mal's most life-changing and influential Bible messages.
- **Plus...** some of Mal's classics, including **lectures to young leaders.**

## ARTICLES

- **Scores of Mal's leadership & topical articles...** on a wide range of subjects.
- **These free articles...** are read regularly by Christians from all around the world.

## ACCESS TO EDGES TV PROGRAMS

- **Many of the *EDGES with Mal Fletcher* programs, which can be  seen in over 210 nations, are now online...** for viewing with either broadband or modem connection.
- **Transcripts and research documents used in the shows...** a unique resource for people who want balanced answers to major social and lifestyle questions.

## NEWS

- **What NEXT WAVE INTERNATIONAL™ is doing...** across Europe.
- **Coming events that you could be part of...** including Master Classes and much more.
- **E-NEWS...** sign up for Next Wave International's™ **free** monthly E-News, with the latest in what's happening in Europe **plus** great articles from Mal.

# BOOKMARK THEM NOW:  ˙

### www.nextwaveonline.com

### www.edges.tv

# YOU
## CAN HELP MAL FLETCHER AND HIS TEAM
### Make a Permanent Impact on Europe!

According to respected Christian leaders like C. Peter Wagner, Western Europe now represents perhaps the darkest region on earth, in spiritual terms.

- Everyday, 30,000 people come to Christ in Latin America.
- Everyday, 25,000 come to Christ in China.
- Everyday, 15,000 come to Christ in Africa.
- Everyday, up to 7,000 people leave the church in Europe!

NEXT WAVE INTERNATIONAL™
is helping to reshape Europe's spiritual future!

**Option 1:**

# GIVE ONLINE...

## IT'S SECURE, FAST & EASY...

# www.nextwaveonline.com

(Use a credit card, direct transfer or Pay Pal account)

## Option 2:

# OR

## USE THE FORM BELOW

YES! I want to help Mal and his international team by investing in this rapidly growing mission across Europe.

Name:_____

Address:_____

Email:_____ Phone:_____

Please debit my:

Visa ☐        Master Card ☐        American Express ☐

Amount  (please include your currency):_____

This is a:

☐ Monthly Pledge        ☐ One-Time Gift

Card No.:  ☐☐☐☐–☐☐☐☐–☐☐☐☐–☐☐☐☐

Name on Card: ——————————————————————

Expiry Date: _____ / _____   Signature: _____

Mail/Fax to:

EUROPE / BRITAIN / USA / CANADA / REST OF WORLD (except *below):
Next Wave International, Drejervej 11-21, 2400 Copenhagen NV, Denmark, Fax: +45-3531-0096


*AUSTRALIA / NEW ZEALAND / ASIA:
Next Wave International, P.O. Box 93, O'Halloran Hill, S.A., 5158, Australia, Fax: +61-8-8322-8101